THOM BOULTON

THE LESSER KEY

STOAT BOOKS

THE LESSER KEY

ISBN: 978-1-918724-01-1

POCKET SERIES

01

First published 2026

Edited by Leona Franke

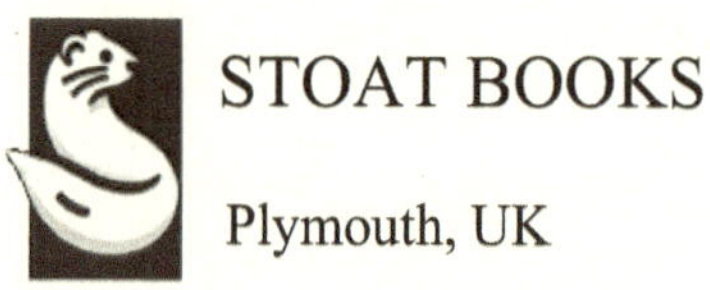

THOM BOULTON

The Lesser Key is a brutal and elegiac reckoning with a world in collapse. Drawing from the language of esoterica, myth, and modern ruin, Thom Boulton crafts poems that speak with the urgency of political sermons and the intimacy of private heresies.

This is a collection shaped by cultural hauntings, absurd revelations, and the grief of witnessing a society unravel through behaviours, rituals, and broken systems. There are no simple redemptions here — only moments of clarity, rage, beauty, and dark laughter carved out from the noise. *The Lesser Key* is not a guidebook for salvation, but a map of where we are now, and what it costs to name it.

OTHER BOOKS:

Prima Materia, 2018

Gebo, 2021

POEMS

THE THURSDAY NIGHT POETRY SALON

And you were there
And you were there
And you were there
And you
    you

    you

this is the Thursday Night Poetry Salon
        its walls lined with torn our
        pages from the books you
        never wrote — about the
        ongoing civil war between the
        uptight and the turned on

        its soft furnishings for your
        aching scrotum, engorged
        labia, and overused arsehole

its queue for the toilet because
some fancy has fascinated the
attention span of aliens and
authors with another long list
of invisible things

its unsaid sayings and
occasional name drop of a
subheading from the New
York Times obituary

this is the Thursday Night Poetry Salon
its haven for those who fled
literary persecution,
misinformation of the
defamation of madness, World
War Three, with roots tied to
the settlement of Three Rivers
City

its host, rite of passage, night
of baptism, this church of the
apocalypse, releasing
outcomes to outcries to
acceptance

its situation, on the corner of a
one-way street, that if you
follow it, will take you from
Hillside to Box — past the
chaos of Plimoth Rock — to
Royal William Carlos
Williams Yard

here at the Thursday Night Poetry Salon
where calls of rebellion are
clothed in the garishness of
prayers and spells

where expectations are exiled
— we horde no currency of
preconception, all things are
real and equally non-existent,
we take our passion by the
waist and waste no time, make
the day and make the bed

where poetic providence lies in
the mechanism of a clock,
charming and chimed, its face
illuminated by the soul of
Three Rivers City, once
raptured and recaptured
following the flood,
following the pale pony

here at the Thursday Night Poetry Salon
where the greater structure
does not understand the time

signature of human emotion,
and pocket realities are the
keys to paradise

where the brothers and mothers
and sisters and fathers of a
forgotten connection, wait —
hell, we hardly knew you

where we are The Man in the
Moon, The Lady in the Lake,
Wooly Bully and Blue Mink,
groundhogs and gremlins
The Ghost of Christmas Past,
all the Kings horses and all the
Kings men, the uptown girls,
twisted fire-starters,
freaks, mutants — and the
eternally reincarnating

where we all dream a republic
but nobody can sleep

from the Thursday Night Poetry Salon
the restless gather to write
revolutionary rhymes but only
manifest crude alliteration —
which exacerbates the
assonance of the whole thing

the philosophers pay their
transcendental taxes by
building beer mat Ouija boards
and burning dandelions to
contact Timothy Leary

the redefining of parameters to
allow moss to grow on your
consciousness and petrify your
body into ash or oak or elder

from the Thursday Night Poetry Salon
the maps of Three Rivers City
are spaced out and drawn on
the backs of each person's
hands — until the only way to
know where you're going is to
form a circle

the gathering great minds stir
their ridiculous notions — all
in an attempt to educate and
entertain — through chaos
magic and storytelling

the years roll into hours, we
explore the inside of our
eyelids, remember the
promises we broke and the
mysticism we forgot

I HAVE EATEN THE DEAD

first published in

International Times, APRIL 2022

*Worm Moon sets

How impressive is the jay
as it leaves no echo in the sky

these eyes search
but have no luck saved up

my focus switches

I watch the clouds passing
to work out the planet's speed

it is very fast today

the disquiet in my stomach
is not motion sickness

but swallowed moonlight

it wriggles, soft like steam

I have eaten the dead for
breakfast

their language and songs
their superstitions

now each one
pinches inside to make my
outside pink

candy-floss coloured feathers

so I may rise
in the fresh air

higher than the jay

leave a trail
so others can find me
sleeping on The Moon

BLOOD-ORANGE

first published in

International Times, JULY 2025

blood orange, blood-hound, the sniff to
whiff out citrus segments

sit this one out chump, the dogs are
coming – the dogs are coming
no, it's just the way they are sitting

sit down next to me, taste this blood
orange, it is different – isn't it? It does
taste different, not like a normal orange

he died as he lived… full of oranges.
Oranges and tea from China, and the
whole set, bone, bone china, give a dog
a bone, blood-hound with a bone, chew,
chew orange slices and peel, and blood-
orange does taste different, not like a
normal orange

RETROGRADE

I want to be so famous
they name a bin after me

I want to be pointed at
because I am known and not not-known

I want coconut milk
blonde hair — and a winter's beach

I want to be a shapeshifter
slim as a ten bob note

I want constellations at war
fighting over my name

I want to be a notch in a lyric
        misquoted custodian of
        imagery

make me pop culture

make me fashionable
then unfashionable

then retro
then retrograde

ahead of the times
out of time
out of sight and out of mind

lose me to the infinity of regret

cast me away in an exile of shame

give me publicised health scares
so that everyone cares if I live or die

give me my own religion
give me dystopias and dynasties

give me my biography so I can regret it
give me my time of death on a receipt

I wanna be associated with a brand
like Siemens or SMEG

I want to blast a constant stream
of music
into my mind to better understand
entropy

I want to be a 1980s New Romantic
because I am an 1890s Old Romantic

I want to kiss daily
and define constantly — a posthuman
love

I want to be clothed
in ghosts and promises

I want to escape the day
bring its ruins with me
as dust in my pocket

I want to be a mirror of your rhyme
a time traveller

I want to know who I am…
I want to know what love is

There's things I don't get
see, I don't recall
ever purchasing gravity
so I must have been born with it

great swathes of the stuff

wrestling with my ego
to keep me grounded

but I don’t want to be bound
by the laws of physics

I was never consulted
about being born
during an apocalypse

television was a poet
crawling towards an Allen Ginsberg
poem

that you can now watch before the
watershed

I want to be an original
    to cheat death
    to cheat at cards

and failing that

I want to write a song that everyone
sings
            at my funeral
            and at their own

my lifeless body orbiting a legacy

and depending on where you're stood
where you view me from
your own motion

it might look like I'm going backwards,
when really

I'm just fashionably late

GARGANTUAN

I heard the snapping of spines — the
seals once fused
to prop up the acropolis of greater
man's marvel

those that fuelled the veins and arteries
of civilisation
filled them with liquid mercury to
measure their fever

they who shunned the masters and
missionaries
and placed marbles in their pockets to
sink deeper

who rebelled against a notion of
notoriety in-exchange for

compromising their natural complexion
and in their turn —
gained notoriety

broke their bellies by ingesting the soup
of chaos and
holding it in, bound in skin and raw
meat, assimilated
through a supplement regiment of zoots
and the fruits of
bass heavy rack

gave with surgical incision their
industrial language, that
lower self, lesser key, trod on the sod
and grasses
of a class system, where the proletaire
demanded profiteroles
haunted by the spectre of communism
now bound and sold

as a children's fable

they who roamed reason and found it
deserted — roasted
by the midday sun and the anarchy of
the moon until they
were caught in the snatch of wild beasts

their sugar-coated growls expelled into
hollow caves
sneaking past the guards of decency —
disguised as an
echo

prophecy is a bomb
constipated

detonates amnesia as alchemy to
transmute ethos

human sacrifice in order to achieve
humanity

THE SELF erupts into ironic glints of
problematic wiles
which indulge THE SELF to liberate
THE SELF

— fucked into existence
— fucked by existence
— fucked

out of their souls, and their minds, and
their bodies, and
their homes, left to breathe the streets of
the imagination
and there conjuring the conjectures of
animated corpses
— enough to garner nods and murmurs
from the widows of

promise, widowed by apathy, lethargy,
leaving no room
for repartee to be processed and
understood

save the second-hand photos from the
charity shop — keep
them alive on an ofrenda made of
offensive heresy
our golden age comic book Jesus Christ
and his arousing hourglass soul —
ready for the beauty pageant

the pageantry of masquerading
totalitarians, the dissolved flesh
of shared truth, our moral and
innocence encouraged into an early
grave
by the fascination of misnomer

this dystopia is autobiographical and
these are indeed dystopian times
it's why the deep state invented George
Orwell (if only there were a term
for plausible deniability) and the over-
subscription to conspiracy and chaos

those with their snapped-spines, left
remanded yet they remain receptive
to the ruminations of the past, resign
themselves to be the
minstrels of madness who will testify in
an open court of sons and daughters
to defend the unseen and unborn

it is not permissible as so often we are
led to believe
the truth?
Six o'clock is too late for coffee but not
to fuck

(keep it in your holster, cowboy)
and God is not one of us, even though
we made him in our image

God loves a cappuccino — takes a stroll
down the road
skips along slabs, buffed and polished
with indifference

catches the scent of bakers shaping
loaves for the Early
Morning rise, loaves made from white-
bred lies and
banker's cocaine — bread so foul even
the ducks won't
chow it down

spies the impossible people lost
between the margins of

the page, ponders over cancel culture
and how they would
have killed Plath or Ginsberg had they
not already been
killed by curiosity

spots bags of hope dumped outside food
banks — signs
reading "feed your babes on dead
butterflies" for nothing
flies in the gravity of this situation

passes the shamanic burning sessions
that erupt in the bars, flaming
spirits rupture reality — everybody's
working for the weekend, where
the banshees wail as they win or lose at
cards — where they fight — this
is where they smoke chokey, cover the
commotion of the locomotive bodies

as they pump their skunk-dust into the
air

watches as they practice smiling
isometric exercises devalued by the lies
of the skulless
(had he made us all jellyfish then we'd
swim)

hears the empty sorries and airing
worries, dried and crinkled
smelling damp, taken in as the night
begins to cough

counts the dropped copies of spiritual
manifestos left bereft on park
benches — there to keep slats warm for
the unhomed swarms who will flock
and forage come twilight's heavy-
tongued kiss

hereby, we find ourselves collecting
data of the celestial experience
where
sentence read backwards is backwards
read sentence
and this life sentence, handed down by
that famous mutant
is nothing more than a loan of time we
cannot pay back

incurable of their honesty — the poetic
warlords declare lore
  that giving to charity is vanity
  that self-citation is an act of love
  that we are the true gods of disco
  that heartache is made of bread and
butter
  that brushes with the law are unjust
and enchanting

that poor is a synonym for rejected
that a clock can't ever catch its breath
that our reasons are dust and late night whispers
that legacy is trapping time in an upturned glass
that your wants are like cracks in the porcelain
that religion is art and art is religion
that God is sick

let cosmological metrics weigh and measure our own divinity
this is GARGANTUAN

this is tardigrades crushed into the lunar surface
choking on silver skin flakes

being promised a glimpse

of brioche from the breakfast table
in a penthouse apartment in New York
Shitty

and if we can't have brioche, we'll have
apples
cut apples, crisp, wet, fresh apples,
carved on tongues
our industrial tongues

our angry tongues

we run our tongues along the ground,
catch gravel in the grooves, chew the
stones and spit into the pit of reason and
revolution

the revolution, presented on the cover of
Reader's Digest and Rolling Stone
Magazine, sell a thousand copies, sell

sword, cellar and cellar door, adored
and in need of a model, the unlocked
potential

the call of the shaman

how we pray for those spiritual
madmen, The Crowley and crackpot, or
Raspy Rasputin and his Mick Jagger-
swagger

those colourful figures, with hand-
painted features — we cannot be
anymore revolting than we already are

are we to be entertained by only the
hazard of politician and pomp

This is bigger
This is THE THEORY OF THE SUN

where we cannot lay siege we will lay
on our backs

see what can happen when you take the
napkin off your lap, wipe
the blood from your mouth and ask to
see the menu

claim back some self-respect — know
the worth of two pennies —
lift your chin, and your hips, and live

before the great minds succumb to the
drummed in affirmations expelled daily
and programmed in through throwaway
phrasing

eat books
read people

for the great temple of love has fallen
— and with it, all our spare change and
newly coined terms

the lord is my shepherd and he has been
caught wanking in the field, the wolves
have come, severed the lanolin from our
bodies — all to be worn like we're
fucking hand puppets

treat the uprising like art and our art like
sex
go bareback and blindside reality —
screaming into the night

we are but the subjects of monsters
we are but the subjects of monsters
we are
we are…

We are dirt We are cringe
We are legion We are knots
We are teeth We are sighs
We are bought and weighed

We are into We are out of
We are deficit of fucks
We are the babes and boom
We are acid jazz We are pop

We are retracted We are redacted
We are synth We are songbird
We are hybrids of time and space
We are leviathans We are kids

We are the dynamos and drums
We are bloody hilarious
We are wrapped up We are under
We are thumbs and thimbles

We are wooden sticks to rub
We are lycra We are velcro
We are limping as we run wild
We are whimpers in the womb

We are greater than our parts
We are in search of the whole
We are talking cum stains
We are receipts for the dead

We are shampoos and soaps
We are canvas We are corporeal
We are creeps We are special
We are ash and its roar

We are more than our membership

We are lightning fast and furious
We are an expulsion of dark matter

We are The Big Bang or Big Bopper
We are the itch and the rains
We are tattoos on the skins of trees
We are rationed We are irrational

We are walkers We are wanderers

PAGAN HOLLYWOOD

At its height **pagan Hollywood** was
fashion

Poseidon and his waves of film
unravelled on the cutting room floor

the graves of those stories littered
between
the roots of silent gods

each director kept a little black book
(a Grimoire)
etched names into the margins
John Lennon and his instant COFFEE
— headliner

at the screening, you talked about
pagan New York

and Joan Didion, like you dreamed it up
yourself — I said
Andy Warhol looked like a cunt

we lived in alternate realities of
meaning, writing
love letters on the backs of our faces

you must have nearly drowned
licking the back of that envelope

hoping for a response

we spent days in a daze
hypnotised by smoke and dogs barking
until the lot emptied
leaving only a conversation of daggers

the Polaroid's on the notice board
replaced by raspberry leaves

and everyone was high on Titanic acid
bought from the backdoor
of a diner filled with minutes

we watched divinity hitch a lift
on the continuity of narrative

watched the velvet dressed nun
filming Bob Dylan kissing Allen
Ginsberg

ate cassette tapes and cigarettes
Buddhism on vinyl
and rock 'n' roll chanted in the temples
at San Francisco
at the ashram Maharishi

aura of paradise
the Technicolor of **pagan Hollywood**

the thrill of your life, champagne
nihilism

betrayed by the symphony of decorum
under a prophetical moon

deny it, your head held face down
on bare knees
bailed out by a tramp in a top-hat
fantastic drugs and alopecia

those freedom fighters
their love letters
lost to destiny — an occult typewriter
all to tackle the mugginess of a reactive
world

and your tree of life
mapped over the paving slabs

exhausted by brightly coloured trousers
and the inevitable death from revelation

as **pagan Hollywood** fell, the larger
questions
emerged from its corpse

forgotten Eden
and the language of the soul
saintly and evolved
deprived of ceremony and mystery
The dead poets are dead
vacant lot and new life squandered
explicit in elicit conduct
morals and ethics enraged

there is no longer scope for symbolic
dimension
it all looks the same from a distance

the running water of the imagination
a moat for the church of the unseen

now put to ruin in the assassination of
culture
and what was shared

in the resurrection of **pagan Hollywood**

the shadows of the beast will curl
ego shall dissolve
as a tablet in the rain

the mysticism of gypsy film will rule
and force those who claim the title of
meek
to renounce the woes of their world

sing out loud the songs of our
mediumship

The Cult of Hanuman and Good Friday
caught out at the soon to be Thursday
Night Poetry Salon

the cosmic homecoming
to The Village, native of earth-spirits
and liquid-dreaming

the chaos bums on their wanderlust
searching for the zeitgeist of quantum
theology
to trap it in a plastic tumbler

every apocalypse a gift
asteroids in retrograde casting spells
and something-something gargantuan
— a fixed scream in time

We are the Third Religion

zealots of the circus
the next show is about to begin
prepare to expose yourself

get some sleep first

a pillow of the novel you wrote
lodged in your rib as you rest on your
side
hurts as you inhale

We are THE MUTANTS of The Third
Religion
sat in Hades, where you can gaze upon
the labyrinth, its centre hidden by a
piece of cake

you are now listening to the warlocks
play their heavy wait

remember **pagan Hollywood** for what it

was —

a golden dawn ritual

now is the time of the cinematic

republic

of **The Blockbuster Age of Mutants**

for the third religion and its book of

psalms

now is the time, the only time

to be incomprehensible

THE THIRD RELIGION

what was dust, takes form

a sacred union

the lesser key shall turn

www.ingramcontent.com/pod-product-compliance
Lightning Source LLC
La Vergne TN
LVHW051021080826
845145LV00009B/2745

* 9 7 8 1 9 1 8 7 2 4 0 1 1 *